YOU CAN BE A WOMAN™ SOFTBALL PLAYER

Sheila Cornell Douty and Judith Love Cohen

Cascade Pass, Inc.

www.cascadepass.com

Editing: Janice J. Wheeler

Published by Cascade Pass, Inc., 4223 Glencoe Avenue, Suite C-105,
Marina del Rey CA 90292-8801 USA
Printed in Hong Kong by South China Printing Co. (1988) Ltd.
First Printing 2000
You Can Be a Woman Softball Player was written by Sheila Cornell Douty and Judith
Love Cohen, and edited by Janice Wheeler. Book design by David Katz, graphics by
Grace Balnis of Grace Graphics.

This book is one of a series that emphasizes the value of sports careers to self-esteem
by depicting real women whose careers provide inspirational role models.
Other books in the series include:
You Can Be A Woman Basketball Player   *You Can Be A Woman Soccer Player*

Library of Congress Cataloging-in-Publication Data
Douty, Sheila Cornell, 1962-
        You can be a woman softball player / Sheila Cornell Douty and Judith Love
Cohen ; -- 1st ed.
                p. cm.
        ISBN 1-880599-47-3 -- ISBN 1-880599-46-5 (pbk.)
        1. Softball for women--Vocational guidance— United States --Juvenile litera-
ture. 2. Douty, Sheila Cornell, 1962---Juvenile literature. 3. Softball players – United
States -- Biography -- Juvenile literature. 4. Women softball players—United States
–Biography—Juvenile literature. [1. Douty, Sheila Cornell, 1962- 2. Softball players.
3. Women—Biography.] I. Cohen, Judith Love, 1933-   . II. Title.

GV881.3 .D68 2000
796.357'8—dc21
[B]
                                                                                        00-020931

Dedication

This book is dedicated by author Sheila Cornell Douty to her mother, Nancy Cornell, who worked and sacrificed for years to provide Sheila with not only an education, but with the highest of standards and morals to take with her. This book is also dedicated to Sheila's Olympic coach, Ralph Raymond, who gave Sheila the inspiration to grow and to be the best she could be, both as a person and as a player.

This book is also dedicated by author Judith Cohen and publisher David Katz to the memory of Katy Colleen O'Harra of Gemini Graphics. Katy provided the encouragment, advice and love that allowed two amateurs to become real book publishers. We never could have done it without her.

It is 1996 in Atlanta, and the baseball stadium is packed with cheering home-town fans. However, the team they're cheering for is not the Atlanta Braves, heading for the World Series, it is "Team USA" in pursuit of the Olympic gold. The opponents, an excellent team from China, are ahead by one run, and the tying run is at bat.

The coach smiles as he looks at his on-deck batter, a very good clutch hitter with a great attitude. He says to her quietly: "Hey Big Girl, how about putting one out?"

Sheila Cornell Douty, alias "Big Girl," is the first baseman on the United States' first women's softball team in the Olympics. The tying run has reached first base as Sheila comes up to bat, and she homers into the center field bleachers. Final score: U. S. 3, China 2.

Team USA went on to win the Olympic gold medal for softball, and Sheila was thrilled at being able to come through for her teammates and her country.

How did Sheila Cornell Douty, an academic All-American who intended to be an orthopedic surgeon, wind up devoting herself full time to playing international softball with Team USA?

How did she find herself surrounded by a coach and teammates, who all felt a oneness with one another? Let her tell us her story, the story of one of a new generation of athletes . . ..

I grew up in the San Fernando Valley in Southern California. I was into everything! I played hard: hide-and-seek, climbing trees, handball, etc. The schoolyard was my favorite place, but I enjoyed what was inside also. I loved math and spelling and reading. I read Nancy Drew mysteries, and when I wasn't playing outside, I usually had a book in my hands. I was also an avid Girl Scout.

My family was close. My mother, grandmother, aunt and two sisters all lived nearby until a year ago when my older sister moved to Sacramento. My mother and aunt were teachers and my younger sister became a teacher. I grew up loving the idea of being good at school and getting a good education, but in the primary grades, I found my attention wandering. I was bored.

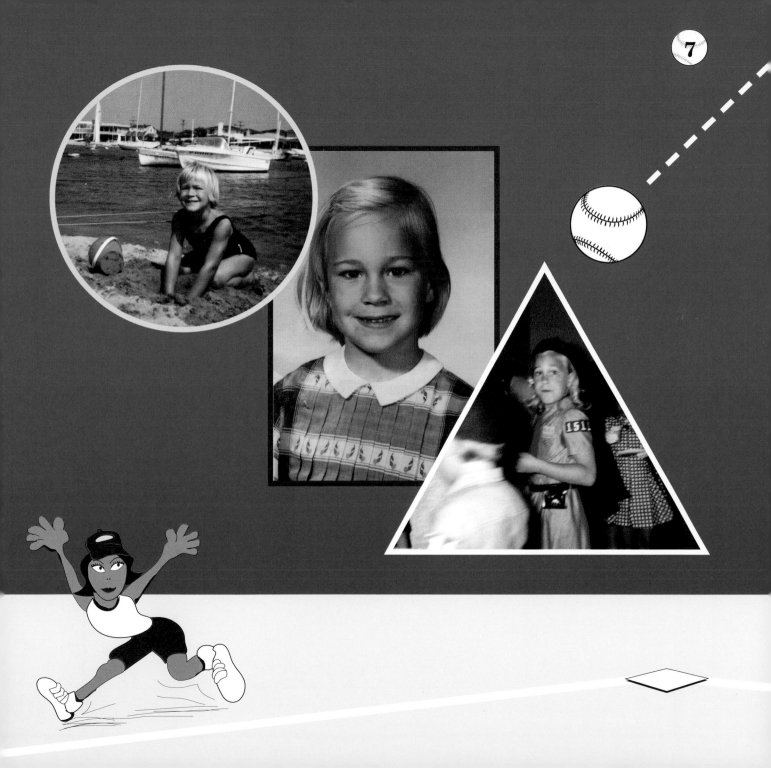

Then my fourth grade teacher changed my future. She had an "open classroom." This meant that when I finished my fourth grade assignments, I was free to move on to other assignments and subjects instead of just waiting for everyone else to catch up. I could follow my interests into new and different areas at my own pace. I advanced in my studies, and was now considered a "gifted" child, instead of a "problem" child.

I dreamed of a future in the medical field. In high school I thought about being an orthopedic surgeon. I was, of course, also very active in various team sports. I worked hard at both sports and academic studies, and was very proud to be accepted at the University of California, Los Angeles (UCLA).

WEST VALLEY
SOCCER
DIV. I
EAGLES
1976

My freshman year at UCLA was very exciting. I was playing softball and volleyball. I was getting a general education and taking psychology, anthropology, political science, mathematics and music.

I thought long and hard about what I wanted to be. I knew I wanted to do something where I could help people make themselves better. I finally selected physical therapy. That meant that I majored in kinesiology and psychology and also studied biology and chemistry. When I graduated, I received department honors of "cum laude" (which means "with praise").

One of my proudest achievements was being named an academic All-American. This honor was important to both me and my family, and ranked right next to my also being inducted into the UCLA Athletic Hall of Fame.

I knew, even before I graduated from UCLA, that I wanted to continue my education and get a master's degree in physical therapy. One of the few schools that offered this program was the University of Southern California (USC), and so I applied for admission and was accepted.

I worked very hard in graduate school, but of course I continued to play softball. In addition to playing in college, I was part of a U.S. team that played in international competition. At one point, I had exams, and I was asked to play softball in Japan. What could I do? My classmates told me I just had to take the tests, but I went to see the director of the physical therapy department. She was wonderful and very supportive. "Of course, you have to play in Japan. Take makeup tests when you get back."

I graduated and went to work as a physical therapist, but what could I do about softball?

It is probably hard for you to believe that while men have played softball for 100 years, it was considered a novelty when, during World War II, women played ball.

While young men were fighting overseas during the war, Philip Wrigley, owner of the Chicago Cubs, backed the All-American Girl's Professional Baseball League in 1943 (as featured in the film "A League of Their Own"). These women usually played fast-pitch softball but for the duration of the AAGPBL, they actually played baseball.

Before I was even born, a player by the name of Dottie Kamenskek was considered the league's best first baseman. Many thought she was better than the men in the major leagues!

The league had team names such as The *Rockford Peaches* and *The Fort Wayne Daisies*. The girls wore skirts, short-sleeved shirts and baseball caps. The league folded in 1954, and it would take over 40 years for women ballplayers to be recognized again.

In 1991, the International Olympic Committee voted to make softball an Olympic event. The players competed to represent the United States by playing in competitions such as the Pan Am games and the 1995 Olympic festival. Fifteen players were selected to represent the United States in the 1996 Olympic games. They included myself as first baseman, Dot Richardson as shortstop, and Lisa Fernandez as pitcher.

My teammates and I are amateur athletes, and therefore do not get payed to play softball. However, there is a Women's Professional Softball League. They play in minor league and college ballparks, and I am looking forward to one day playing professional softball.

I love the game of softball. There is very little luck involved; it is a game of skill. The objective of the game is for a team (nine players) to score more runs than an opposing team in seven innings. The defense tries to get three outs as quickly as possible and therefore prevent the other team from scoring.

In softball, the distance between the bases is only 60 feet, instead of 90, as in baseball. Fielders must have lightning quick reflexes in order to make the plays. Softball pitchers are only allowed to throw an underhanded pitch from 40 feet away. The balls are heavier and larger than the ones used in baseball. And the fences are much closer.

The positions are the same nine positions found in baseball:

Position 1. The pitcher needs to consistently throw the ball over the plate and change speeds on pitches to keep batters off balance.

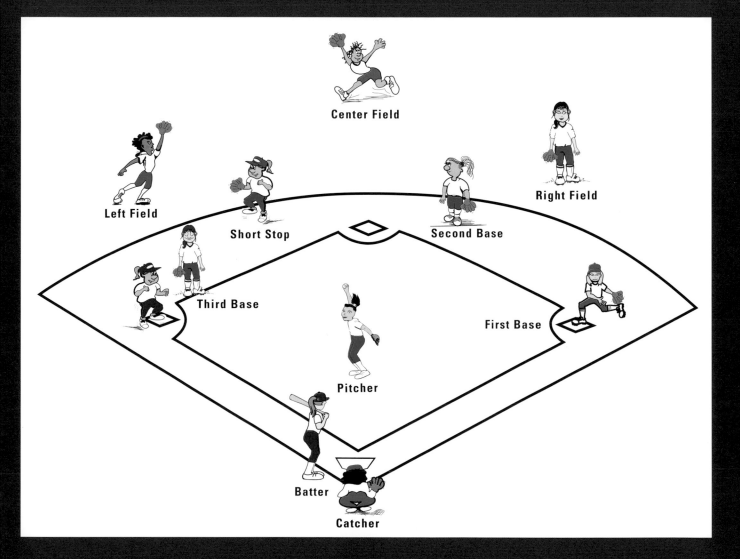

Position 2. The catcher crouches behind home plate and must be fearless, quick and have a good arm to be able to throw out runners at all bases.

Positions 3-6. The infield has four players: 1st , 2nd , and 3rd basemen and a short-stop. These players need good reflexes, fast footwork and good arms. The shortstop usually has the best range in covering the area, and the 3rd and 1st baseman usually have especially quick reflexes.

Positions 7-9. The outfield has three players: left-, right- and center- fielders. They cover a lot of ground and, they too need good arms to throw with speed and accuracy.

In order to be a successful position player, you need to be focused on teamwork. Go out and watch games or videos before you select the position you want to play. Or perhaps your coach can recognize your unique talents and suggest the best position for you to play.

After I graduated from USC, I worked as a physical therapist in California from Labor Day to Memorial Day, and during the softball season I played for the Raybestos Brakettes in Stratford Connecticut

But in 1994, I was fortunate to be able to train full-time for the Olympic team. Now, throughout the year we play in North, Central or South America during the Pan American Games; in Australia or New Zealand for the South Pacific Classics; in Japan, China, Korea, or a number of other countries including the U.S. at International Softball Federation (ISF) games. When we are not playing, we are working on our conditioning with speed, agility and quickness training, or we are on the field practicing our fielding and our hitting.

It is wonderful to share this experience with my coach and my teammates.

In the off-season I work with kids at softball camps and clinics, teaching them to hit, field or to throw.

I love to talk to kids in schools and at camps and to softball coaches at clinics. Because of the phenomenal growth of the sport of softball, there is a tremendous interest and a demand for speakers. So many young girls want to start playing the game of softball, and they are the future of our sport.

I share with them all how much fun it is. Why else would you want to play if it wasn't fun? But there is more: the feeling of hitting the ball, the sense of being there with your coach and your teammates, the friendships you build, the confidence and self-esteem that you gain. If I can help to motivate young girls in the game of softball and the game of life, and encourage them to always be the best they can be, then I am rewarded.

How can you tell if you would be good at softball? If you can answer yes to the following questions, then you should consider becoming a softball player.

1. Are you patient and willing to work to make yourself better, to practice harder?

Softball is a game of skill: hitting pitches, fielding balls, throwing balls and running bases. Learning all these requires lots of practice in order to do it just right every time.

2. Are you interested in working on your physical conditioning and strength? Are you willing to sometimes give up spending time with your non-team friends and play or practice instead?

In order to be able to hit and run and throw for hours at a time, you need to be in good physical condition. This requires additional hours of weight-lifting and running.

3. Are you able to work as a team member, being cooperative, willing and able to sacrifice for the common goal of the team?

Teamwork is the very heart of softball. No game is ever won because of one player, no matter how great that player is. As a first baseman, I usually cannot get a player "out" unless one of my infielders fields the ball first and then throws it to me. In order for me to hit the winning run in the Olympic game against China, I needed my teammate to get on base. In order for us to win the game, our pitcher and defense had to do their jobs and get the Chinese batters out. My teammates and coach are like family to me, and working with them is one of the greatest joys of my life.

What I like best about my career as a softball player is that playing the game gives me self-confidence. I also learn self-discipline when I practice a skill on which I need to improve. Most of all, I like playing the game because of the pure joy I feel. Playing is fun.

I get to use various skills that I learned at some point in life: as an umpire in the park leagues I learned the rules of the game, which is always helpful in actually playing the game; as a woman athlete I had to decide how to pursue my sports career while working and going to school; today, as an athlete representative working with the national Olympic team, I can help future Olympic athletes receive better training and financial support.

And our year 2000 Olympic softball team has eleven returning players! These are my teammates from 1996!

My future goals are:

I want to continue to play softball, this time professionally in the new Women's Professional Softball League (WPSL).

I want to continue to work with children in camps and clinics. Everyone has special skills. I want to help kids find out what they do best.

I want to continue to work with the Olympic team, helping with the selection of players. I also want to help improve the opportunities for the young athletes that will come after me.

If you want to always strive to make yourself better, to constantly practice your skills and keep yourself in top physical condition; if you want to compete together with your teammates at the best competitive level of your sport; and if you want to work with those teammates for a common goal, then you can do it too. You can be a woman softball player.

YOU CAN BE A WOMAN SOFTBALL PLAYER

SOFTBALL CLINIC ACTIVITY 1

PURPOSE: Learning to keep your eye on the ball.

MATERIALS: Colored markers and a bucket of balls.

PROCEDURES: Prior to activity, the leader draws one color circle, the size of a quarter, on each ball. Use several different color markers. Then the balls are mixed in the bucket. One child is the tosser, and one of the other children is the fielder. The tosser reaches into the bucket and randomly selects a ball and tosses it. The fielder must call out the color on each ball as they are fielding the ball.

CONCLUSIONS: It is essential that fielders *keep their eyes on the ball.*

SOFTBALL CLINIC ACTIVITY 2

PURPOSE: To practice sacrifice bunting, a skill needed to advance a runner into scoring position.

MATERIALS: Bat, balls, five cones or markers.

PROCEDURES: Place cones in five different locations in front of the batter. The pitcher pitches a ball to the batter at the plate who squares and sacrific bunts, attempting to get the ball to stop rolling at each of the cones. Pitch ten balls to each batter. The batter gets one point for each cone she touches.

CONCLUSIONS: Batters need to learn to control bunts in order to place them where they need to be to advance a runner.

SOFTBALL CLINIC ACTIVITY 3

PURPOSE: Learning bat control and getting the barrel of the bat into the ball.

MATERIALS: Bat, two or three balls.

PROCEDURES: Have the batter stand 15 feet from fielders.
Fielders are lined up in a row. One fielder tosses the ball to batter who takes an easy swing working on getting head of bat into the ball. Fielder fields it then tosses to the batter again. Hitter should try to control bat and swings so that she hits to each fielder, one after the other. Batter takes 12 to 15 swings, then switches with fielders who rotate.

CONCLUSIONS: Players need eye/hand coordination, bat control, and fielding skills. Batters need to be able to control where the ball goes.

About the Authors:

Sheila Cornell Douty is now a member of the United States Women's Softball Olympic team. Prior to this, she attended University of California, Los Angeles where she played spectacular softball (Pac-10 All-Decade team and induction into UCLA's Athletic Hall of Fame) while earning her bachelor's degrees in kinesiology and psychology. At the University of Southern California she continued to play internationally while earning her master's degree in physical therapy. While working as a physical therapist, she also played for the Stratford CT Raybestos Brakettes and the California Commotion. Sheila recently took up skiing and lives in Southern California with her husband, Joel, and her youngest step-son, Bryan, and occasionally gets to play with her step-granddaughter, Alexis.

Judith Love Cohen is a Registered Professional Electrical Engineer with bachelor's and master's degrees in engineering from the University of Southern California and University of California at Los Angeles. She has written plays, screenplays, and newspaper articles in addition to her series of children's books that began with You Can Be a Woman Engineer.

Acknowledgements:

Maxine Lachman for research and contributions on the topic of women's sports.

Photographs by various sources researched and supplied by Women' Sports Services:
Copyright © 1996 Jerry Ballas, two photos pgs.3, 15;
Copyright © 1996 ALLSPORT USA RUSTY JARRETT, pgs. 17, 21, 31;
Nancy Cornell pgs. 5, 7, 9,11,13, 23, 25;
Brant R. Bender .... www.phoenixphotography.com pgs. 27, 29, 33, 35, and covers.

A portion of the proceeds of this book will be donated to the WISC Foundation (Women in Sports Careers), a non-profit foundation which provides skills and tools to encourage and retain girls and women of all ages in sports-related careers. For more information, go to www.wiscfoundation.org.